PERCUSSION! WOODWINDS! AND BRASS! MY! OH MY!

Percussion!

Woodwinds!

and

BRASS!

MY! OH, MY!

Dr. Paul E. Rosene

Sea-Hill Press Inc.

Printed in the United States of America.

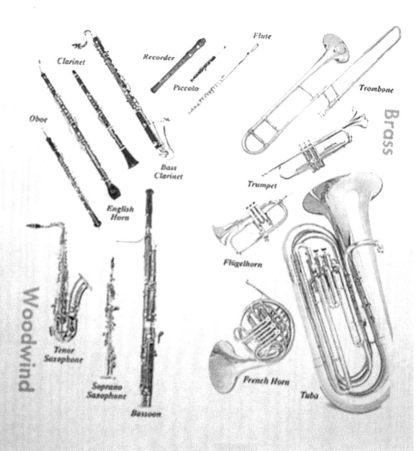

Clarinet

Recorder

Flute

Piccolo

Trombone

Brass

Oboe

Bass
Clarinet

Trumpet

English
Horn

Flügelhorn

Woodwind

Tenor
Saxophone

Soprano
Saxophone

Bassoon

French Horn

Tuba

Dedication

This little book is dedicated to the memory of my wife, one of the first female school BAND DIRECTORS in the state of Illinois. She passed away in August 2020.

A wonderful wife and a very accomplished musician, friend, teacher, and mentor.

God has blessed her!

She is missed! May her memory linger on and on!

—Her husband, Paul

Mrs. Doris M. Rosene

Contents

Dr. Paul E. Rosene

To the young (or new) school BAND director

Forewarned!

This section explains the little book you are reading. The book is NOT designed to offer fingering charts or arrangements for your BAND. Rather, it is designed and then prepared to assist you in the necessary discipline and development of orderliness and emotional responses from your students during BAND rehearsals!

Remember YOU are teaching young learners! *Individual* students who need to have interesting and compassionate Teachers/ Directors who fully *understand* them as they learn.

Your BAND learners look up to you for proper guidance and techniques to develop a real direction in their lives. So, this little book offers a compilation of teaching ideas that can be of assistance as you develop your BAND into a unit of emotional products to your audiences . . . a BAND of which you will be very proud!

The benefits of all this?

**YOU WILL RECEIVE RECOGNITION
FOR YOUR FINE TEACHING!**

May God bless your efforts and may you make a beautiful and correct musical experience for both your BAND students and their many audiences!

Dr. Paul E. Rosene

Dr. Paul and Doris Rosene, School Band Directors

Foreword

The author is well-versed in the subject of this little book!

Dr. Rosene has more than fifty years' experience teaching music, as a public school BAND director, then teaching in the U.S. Air Force Band school and later as a University BAND director/music educator.

He has taught music on all levels of public school and more than twenty-five years as a University Professor, preparing university students for a career as a school BAND director.

An explanation:

This is NOT a book of instruction for the detailed methods of fingerings and/or specific methods for each of the many BAND instruments, for the author is convinced that the reader has already completed university courses in BAND instruments and perhaps earned a degree!

Rather this little book offers suggestions, ideas and anecdotes used to illustrate common-sense sequences that can enhance the music student's learning, which then may be the catalyst for the young BAND director's progress toward successful and productive teaching techniques.

ENJOY!

Chapter One: **Percussion!**

What? Why do you begin this book with Percussion?

Do you believe that you understand?

The most overlooked and undeveloped section in the school BAND is the Percussion section! Yes, from my many years both directing and judging school BANDS from several states, I always seem to find problems ... problems that could have been easily solved by the BAND director during any regular rehearsal time!

For instance: Precision! Yes, I said "PRECISION"

Why are so many school BAND Percussion sections lacking in accuracy and precision?

During my time teaching students and then directing Student Teaching experiences of future BAND directors, I have observed many BAND rehearsals led by a new student or young BAND director. When the rehearsal was finished, I would ask about the Percussion section players. I ask about the students playing the instruments.

Yes, the students!

Did the young teacher notice that the snare drummer's grip was inaccurate? Did the young teacher see the score ... why was the "Gong" not played? AND, why didn't you say something to the triangle player when the instrument was not held correctly? AND, did you really realize that the entire section was not precise ...

none of them were matching your conducting gestures?

The point is that the young directors just simply seem to ignore the Percussion section during rehearsals! Yes . . . they ignore the students! Many times, after the rehearsal is completed I would ask: "Why did you ignore the students in the Percussion section when they missed so many things? Did you actually see the notes in the score?" WHAT? . . . You **WHAT?**

WHY NOT?

All Percussion players and all the players in the BAND must understand the importance of precision! When PRECISION is finally reached, you will soon notice a calming of the Percussion section players. Pride seems to just "jump out" when everything is accurate and precise!

Congratulations! Now think next time and actually strive to achieve accurate Precision!

NOW, on to the ancillary instruments . . .

The Cymbals must be held correctly and then properly played. Hold one cymbal still and move the other up and down. Learn to control the intensity of the sound! Be fully prepared to play the cymbals in a soft manner when you see the *"pp"* marks! DO IT, and insist that the cymbalist completely understands how and why!

Now on to the Xylophone and/or Bells player: Always position the player and instruments in the BAND set-up to be absolutely certain they can SEE the director as they are playing! Hold the mallets correctly with the back of the hand up toward the ceiling and the fingers and thumb holding the shaft of the mallet. WATCH them during the playing and then offer corrections and/or praise! Be verbal with all students!

Snare and Tenor Drums: Hand positions and sticks/mallets held correctly? Are the drums tuned with accuracy? Check the tension rods for the sound YOU desire . . . all tenors must be tuned together. Listen with care to the snare drums, and teach the players to listen and then properly adjust all tension rods. Glockenspiel and other percussion students need to be carefully and properly played. Check postures and hand positions constantly!

All Percussionists must stand when playing. Insist! Watch for correct and erect posture. Backs straight and shoulders back. Their "look" must be of confidence, calm and professional. *(The only exception to be made is for the JAZZ or SWING Drum SET player ... that player can remain seated.)*

Other Percussion instruments, such as the Gong, Triangle, and other sounds must be played with accurate technique! Never discipline, "put to shame" or offer negative feelings about any student's playing. Discuss techniques with them in a conversational and professional manner.

Techniques are most important to the composer of the music being played, so they are most important to your BAND. Play all percussive instruments properly and always, ALWAYS compliment the players when everything is done properly!

When your BAND is in the "marching" mode, instruct the section very carefully in the "street beat" patterns and then begin to offer modes of SILENCE which can offer interesting sounds ... activities within the BAND to watching and listening audiences! Often, I would have the Percussion just play a very basic beat to provide variety in the "marching scheme."

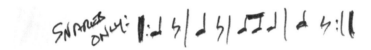

When all BAND members continually and are accurately "in step" begin to provide other experiences in emotion as your BAND members march and play. Following several sequences of the above "system" and perhaps even marching in silence, suddenly EXPLODE the area with total and complete Percussion SOUNDS! ... Have the entire section play a very special beat sequence or have the BAND play a short sequence of big chordal changes ... all of which will provide a new and emotional effect!

When marching, always vary the cadence sounds, systems, section played, etc.! Attempt to always, and at each marching function, offer an unusual sequence of Percussion sounds. Perhaps you might even ask your BAND members to just march a full sixteen bar cadence in _complete_ silence! **WOW!** THAT effect will surprise and please your Parade Audiences!

This sound/silence/sound system can be used to keep your audience interested in the "difference" that YOUR BAND creates from other bands in the marching scene. Consider it, teach it, and present it to your audiences. It is also suggested that you MIGHT use that same technique as an "encore" to any indoor Concert presentation or use it just prior to an intermission!

Always teach _pianissimo (pp)_ sections very carefully. Your BAND students are not aware of the physical problems that must be solved when playing their instruments in very soft manner. Use and produce very proper breath controls and support . . . check with everyone in your BAND for proper breath support of all tones. Practice long phrases and ask your Percussion students to stand and breathe with the BAND members. KNOW that _everyone_ in the BAND should know HOW to control one's breath support when playing long phrases . . . and when to actually breathe in a new supply of air! Teach that concept to the Percussion section, too! That basic requirement is to be made very clear to all BAND members.

Now begin to work on BALANCE. Are the Percussion players really watching and producing the sound to match your Conducting motions? Are your conducting motions accurate for the score you are reading? What dynamics are to be played? Are all Percussion players following your motions? Can you expect _pianissimo (pp)_ passages from the Percussionists? Insist and practice very soft playing.

Are all special percussive effects being played? Be certain that snare drummers are very, VERY, accurate. Do Not allow them to ignore dynamic marks. Do not allow effects to be "false," but work diligently on the creative effects desired in the score!

Hold Cymbals correctly and when played, be certain that only ONE cymbal is moving. Be fully aware of the student's motions. Know how to roll with mallets when called for in the score. Evenness is the secret. Insist on correct playing with the Cymbal roll!

The BASS Drum should be tilted at a 60 degree angle. Lift the Bass drum sound OUT of the instrument. Do not pound it in! Help your Bass Drummer to use the proper technique . . . lift the mallet away from the drum when playing!

Triangle should be held high—about shoulder/head high!—for accurate triangle tone . . . hold the instrument with one hand and play it using a correct beater, with the other. Can the player "roll" easily and correctly? Help your triangle player to fully understand this most important role. Work at it!

Other percussive effects must be played with finesse! Hold maracas high, which always brings a real "lift" to the entire BAND sound. Be aware of correct positions and sound of EACH Percussion instrument and then **KNOW HOW AND THEN DO!**

My Notes

Chapter Two: **Woodwinds!**

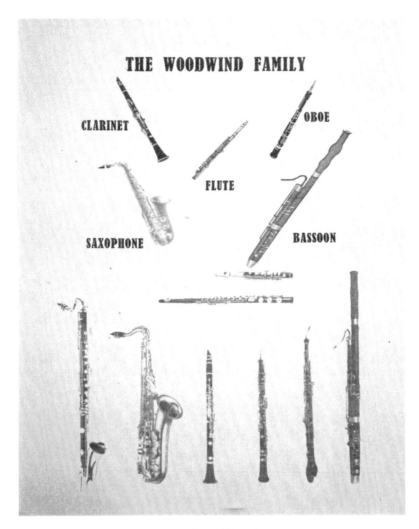

Woodwind Family

The school BAND Woodwind section typically includes: Piccolos, Flutes, Soprano Bb Clarinets, Oboes, Bassoons, and Saxophones. The Eb Clarinet, The Alto, Bass and Contra-Bass Clarinet and Contra-Bassoon are often added. The Concert BAND's Woodwind section is normally much larger and more diverse than in an Orchestra.

The main distinction between woodwinds is in the manner of producing the sound. The Piccolo and Flute are played by splitting the airstream across the tone hole which causes the airstream to vibrate and thus produce the sound.

All single reed woodwinds: Clarinets and Saxophones, utilize single reed systems into the opening of the mouthpiece (using a ligature to secure the reed in position). When the breath is forced between the reed and the mouthpiece, the reed causes the air column to vibrate and then produces its unique sound.

The Oboe and Bassoons produce their sound by blowing air into and through a double reed system. Often, instead of metal, the Piccolos and Flutes might be made of wood, although all Saxophones are created with metal bodies.

All right, you have created your Woodwind section into various parts: Flutes in front rows in a semi-circle system. First Flutes to your RIGHT, so that they play toward and into the BAND set up. The Second Flutes are played to your LEFT, so they play out and towards the audience. Keep the Melody Flutes (first part) into and toward the BAND set-up and the second part Flutes playing toward the audience. Maintain ALL Flutes in a horizontal position when playing.

Soprano Bb Clarinets to your left, seated immediately behind the second Flute section. First Clarinet part in front, second Clarinet part in the next row followed by the third and fourth part in successive rows. Always BALANCE the section by playing more players on the third and fourth parts, with no more than four on the second part and keep the first part with the less numbered players.

Oboes and Bassoon sections should be placed in the BAND set-up and as close to the center as possible.

Position your Alto, Bass, and Contra-Bass Clarinets next to the Saxophones section. Always provide a stand for the Baritone Saxophone player's instrument. Young players need to have the security of a stand … develops confidence!

Watch your Woodwind players to assure that they all produce correct mouth positions. All jaws should be down and the mouth open. Keep the sides of the mouth firm. When playing, all Clarinet players must hold their instruments close to the body.

Watch carefully that all sections are correct in every manner. Offer only constructive criticism when you see errors. Never use discipline or "negative" comments to your BAND. Develop full confidence among your players … with confident comments!

As relative new instruments, invented and produced, are the Saxophones. The Saxophones were invented about 250 years ago!

While typically constructed of metal (brass) the Saxophone is actually a member of the Woodwind family because it uses a reed to produce its distinctive sound. The sound is produced when the player's embouchure creates an airtight seal over the mouthpiece and that player's air stream vibrates a single reed much in the manner of a Clarinet.

Despite the previous comment that the Saxophone is usually made of brass, there are a some exceptions: some models are made of bronze, copper or even sterling silver! A few models of plastic Saxophones have been made over the years. Acrylic plastic Alto Saxophones were quite popular, with their bodies made of "state of the art" injection-molded plastic, with all keys made of metal.

Although wood is preferred for all Woodwind mouthpieces, some plastic mouthpieces might be provided, for they are easy to make, durable and inexpensive.

Offer suggestions to your students to control the sound of any Woodwind instrument. Be careful of the reeds and always insist that all players of Woodwind instruments utilize new reeds or the one in use should be in perfect condition.

Work your young BAND Woodwind section to develop a unified sound to adequately create the proper balance needed from this large section of your school BAND.

My Notes

Chapter Three: **Brass!**

TRUMPETS AND CORNETS: Should be seated behind the Soprano Clarinet Section Never put more than three players on the FIRST part; nor more than four players on the second part and the remaining players of your section on third and fourth parts!

Watch all players for correct posture; all must sit erect and backs straight and away from the backs of the chairs. Consider using STOOLS instead of standard chairs if the players in the Trumpet/Cornet section seems to "slump" regularly.

Embouchures should be proper and secure. Instruments must be held in a level position when playing. Instruct students to properly utilize the "saliva valve" often, to avoid any unusual sounds to emanate.

Keep all instruments clean and allow *nothing* in the instrument cases, except:

an EXTRA mouthpiece
an EXTRA valve oil bottle
a STRAIGHT mute
a cleaning cloth
(Select a very reliable and competent Section Leader!)

FRENCH HORNS: If at all possible, all French horn players should be placed directly near the BASS section. Periodically check the RIGHT hand positions inside the bell for the hands should be "cupped" to adequately produce the traditional tone color. Always listen carefully for this tone color and work to for its eventual achievement. Encourage ear training exercises for all hornists and then compliment them when correct pitches are achieved!

Place the first part player to the left of the section.

Should you have mellophones, check their left hands for the proper "cupped" position. Attempt to achieve a somewhat similar tone for the proper "balance" with the French horns.

BARITONE AND EUPHONIUMS: Be certain that all players backs are not touching the backs of the chairs when playing. Then check to be absolutely certain that the instruments are being held in an erect position and that the sound produced is clear. Encourage a big and sonorous tone color!

Compliment all Baritone and Euphonium players often during rehearsals! Always encourage . . . to develop confidence!

TROMBONES: This section should always be placed behind other sections, usually to the director's right. Trombones should blow "through" the rest of the BAND. No more than two players on the first part; no more than three on the second part, and the rest of the section should be assigned to the third and fouth parts. BALANCE. Watch for proper playing positions and when playing, always encourage ALL Trombones to keep the instrument slides level with the floor!

When producing tones on the trombone, both elbows should be positioned away from the body during playing. Check to assure that only the thumb and first/second finger of the right hand is used to move the slide mechanism. You might always encourage all the trombonists to engage in advanced ear training exercises to develop consistent and correct pitch awareness within the section. Avoid extreme distances in slide position movement when using vibrato. Keep it close and keep it simple!

TUBAS AND BASS HORNS: If your students are small and/or very young, I encourage stands be used to support the instruments securely. Encourage the correct positions of the instruments, for it is most important to properly achieve the total "true" sound of the Bass line. You need to develop firm and consistent players for all Bass line instruments.

Keep fingers fully curved over the several valve mechanisms

and do NOT allow the third/fourth finger to be "pulled back" as the bass line is played.

Cleanliness is most important; therefore, encourage opening and using the "saliva valve" often, to keep the bass sound clear and consistent. Double check to ensure that the instrument bells are positioned forward and toward the podium. When recruiting for the Bass line players, encourage those apparently undecided students to select the Tuba and/or Bass Horn as their choice as they learn to play a BAND instrument.

Work rehearsals for bass line precision. Play "together" very accurately and insist! Practice clarity of sound and double check that all bass players are tonguing clear and precise.

(DO NOT allow players of the low Brass instruments to consistently slur all their notes! Read the music accurately!)

Encourage confidence and develop a consistent ability to produce a dynamic range between the very soft ("pp"), passages and the very loud ("ff") parts. Work that ability at many rehearsals by playing different passages with different dynamic ranges. Work the entire BRASS sections for accuracy, balance, clarity, and absolute precision.

To Check Entire Brass Section:

Trumpets/Cornets held horizontally? All Fingertips on valve caps? Tonguing clear and correct? Saliva valve used often? Encourage full and sonorous tones always played well and with jaws down!

French horns should be checked for right hand positions. They all must keep the left arm up and toward the front with their thumb on top, holding the instrument away from the body. Check jaws for that full and open sound . . . to avoid the "crushed" tones commonly played. Encourage long and well supported phrasing.

Trombones and Baritone Horns should always produce a big and robust sound. Jaws down when playing. Check slide positions for accurate tuning.

BAND accuracy is found in the Tuba Bass horn section. Big and well supported tones … open mouth with jaws down when playing. Balance total sound with your BAND. The bass sounds should prevail. Work at it!

General Characteristics of
All Brass Instruments:

Of the many wind instruments, those called "BRASS" are perhaps the most closely interrelated as far as tone production. Embouchures and acoustical characteristics are all basically very similar. A discussion of those characteristics common to all BRASS instruments might be helpful toward the full understanding of certain points.

TONE PRODUCTION: The principle of tone production in all Brass instruments is the lip or lips … peculiar to the Brass family of instruments. It is characterized by the vibration of the lip or lips which sets the sound in motion. One might describe the lip as the "generator," the length of tubing of the instrument as the *"resonator,"* and the bell as the *"amplifier."*

EMBOUCHURE: It is necessary that all Brass players be carefully selected and motivated to learn. The successes of the embouchure formation will be the reason for actual success! The degree of flexibility and muscular texture of the lip will be the reason for success or failure in playing. As it is believed, only by testing the future Brass student can be the medium of success to be fully assured. There are two main systems: The individual size of the child will dictate the vertical position of the mouthpiece on the lips. Try to center the mouthpiece on the lips. Usually, the most natural and most comfortable position is best. However, when assisting **French Horn** players, usually about two-thirds of the upper placement of the lip is considered proper. Always place the mouthpiece in the center of the lip formation. Tension will govern the speed of vibration and therefore the pitch produced. Have the child "buzz" the lips. When the tension is increased, the upper lip muscles should focus to the center, NOT to the corners of the lips.

The lower lip is responsible for adjusting the size of the opening. As the pitch rises, the lower lip may slightly rise in the center, decreasing the size of the opening. When the pitch becomes lower, the opening becomes larger.

The center of the lips is responsible for vibration and size of the opening. The player must learn to adjust the lips appropriately for the pitch desired. In forming the embouchure for a pitch in the medium range, the player might just think to blow a thin stream through the center on a very cold day. The opening of the lips is similar to the hub of a wheel, with the lip muscles as the spokes all pointing toward the hub!

The corners of the mouth are to be pulled back slightly. Corners must always be firm and held in a stationary position. However, they must never be hard, or even tense! Always achieve to produce a full and sonorous tone, avoiding a thin sound and/or lack of flexibility.

ACOUSTICAL CHARACTERISTICS: All the Brass family of instruments are closely related by similar acoustic principles. Notice that the chart below indicates that the instruments overblow the partials above the fundamental pitch. This chart indicates the range of the instrument up to the eighth partial.

A characteristic common to all Brass instruments is that of pitch changes as affected by temperature changes. Pitch in all Brass instruments might change as the warmer the temperature in the instrument, the pitch produced becomes higher! The colder temperature in the instrument, the pitch produced will become lower!

My Notes

Chapter Four: **Rehearsal Techniques**

Dr. Rosene Conducting

CONDUCTING IS AN ART FORM!

Remember that fact! Conducting a rehearsal is truly an _ART_ form. Conducting is NOT beating rhythms, nor offering fingerings correctness. It is truly interpreting the creators of the scores; what was their wishes? Always plan to produce an emotional reaction by playing the music, both from your BAND members and the audiences who hear your BAND.

Keep your left arm/hands/face toward the various sections for proper cueing and expect to produce an emotional experience! Keep your right arm/hand for rhythm correctness.

Arms/hands/face contortions toward the individual BAND section you are cueing; and always expect to hear and receive an emotional contact from them. They may only know what has been thought/taught to them! Therefore, speak about it, explain the passage, and tell them what you expect them to do! Use words that are easily understood and clear to the young mind. Discuss with them what you hope to achieve, so that they know what is happening! . . .

or, WHAT SHOULD BE HAPPENING!

The young mind is eager to learn. However since you are teaching a non-verbal subject:

MUSIC,

therefore, you must explain fully the meanings in the score; read the notes clearly given and the words listed to help interpret the meaning of the composer/arrangers work. KNOW THE BEAT FLOW AND RHYTHMIC PATTERNS! Never forget that the young musician

"ONLY KNOWS WHAT HE KNOWS!"

In other words, "he knows only what he has been taught." Many young BAND members are unable to interpret the music given to them . . . that competency is up to YOU to teach and guide them into full understanding!

Yes, YOU, the rehearsal conductor of MUSIC, must guide and explain the score. TEACH, by speaking explanations of the music! Interpret the words you have just used by the motions of your conducting technique! Teach via body/hands with your motions . . . always what the score is indicating to you!

JUST DO IT!

When your young BAND students begin to fully understand and to facilitate your conducting motions with their accurate playing AND when they begin to fully understand what YOU are doing, recognizing your capability as a informer/musician, then and ONLY THEN will your group begin to fully come together and make real music happen!

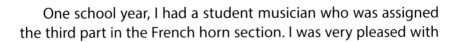

One school year, I had a student musician who was assigned the third part in the French horn section. I was very pleased with that section, for I had four truly outstanding musicians playing!

I was directing one of Elgar's marches and as I was interpreting, I began to hear notes not written in the score. The notes were played well, but certainly not notes written by Elgar! I was baffled at first, but remained calm. I was considering many things to do, but one thing was certain: I HAD to find and/or expose that "problem" to solve this very unusual situation!

I stopped the BAND and told them to begin again at letter "B" and then keep playing. I told them that I would leave the podium during their playing and walk inside the BAND setup.

The BAND began to play at letter "B" an as I walked through the BAND set-up, I heard those same "different" notes again! They were correct pitches, certainly fitting within the chords sequences, but certainly not the notes desired by the composer! Where and what student was doing that?

I continued walking within the BAND set-up and moved toward the French Horn section. What was that I hear? The student playing the third part was improvising with "other notes." I listened carefully and realized that the students playing the First, Second, and Fourth parts were playing properly!

I stopped the BAND and indicated that we would begin again at the beginning. I had found the problem!

WOW!

What to do? I was pleased with that student, for he could play notes on pitch and "fit in" with the composer's intentions. All right, I will follow my thoughts. I asked that French Horn player to stay a moment after BAND rehearsal.

When the young musician remained, to obey my instructions, I offered compliments on the musicianship and innovative techniques he exhibited in his playing! I truly was pleased, in a way, that the French Horn player was innovative, using original and his own thoughts as we rehearsed the BAND. But, I had to question the actions! The notes he played, although accurate with the specific chords, did not "fit" the composer's intent at all! As I questioned and explained, it was admitted that the "improvising" within that music was all his fault! As I further explained the purposes of rehearsal, he admitted his actions and agreed to stay with the part assigned and to play it "as written."

(Following his graduation from High School and several years later that young musician became a composer, now contributing to the music world successfully!)

————————O————————

As a young conductor, you must correct problems as they occur. Do it firmly and quickly, or the offender will repeat the same act over and over! Read the "tidbits" later in this book, which present specific problems with possible solutions Keep track of the "solutions" YOU achieve during your career. I heartily recommend it!

MY GENERAL COMMENTS TO THE MEMBERS OF THE BAND:

Have faith in God and in your abilities!

Work toward . . . *always* . . . work toward success in everything you do! Say words of confidence to yourselves and the truth of making great music happen. Never be afraid or cautious to ask for advice! Your young mind is wide open for you to learn and observe and gain knowledge in many fields! Fill it up with wisdom and carefully presented comments to others to portray your true leadership!

Never hesitate to speak to your young learners! Reinforce in YOUR mind over and over that "YOUR STUDENTS ONLY KNOW WHAT THEY HAVE BEEN TAUGHT!" An amazing statement, yes but very true!

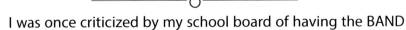

I was once criticized by my school board of having the BAND play "complicated music, such as symphonies. Why do you do such things . . . just play marches! Your audiences would enjoy that."

I was astounded, but told the board and my Superintendent, **"You hired me to come to come to your community to raise the musical standards. AND . . . that your children should learn to play well. I can and will do that for you."**

After hearing my words, the school board or Superintendent never criticized me again!

That is the type of confidence factor that I wish for you!

YOU CAN DO IT!

I wish you great and continued successes! May God bless you, the reader of this little book!

Dr. Paul E. Rosene

My Notes

Chapter Five: **Beginning Sequences**

Mrs. Doris M. Rosene teaching and mentoring her French horn section.

BEGIN THE REHEARSALS . . .
THE TECHNIQUES

TUNE . . . Tune . . . TUNE

Begin all rehearsals with a form of scales and/or chorales to encourage LISTENING and follow through with a carefully planned system of Tuning!

> "A skillful director may, and often does, offer a clever and functionally useful statement during a rehearsal moment, usually on a subject in which yesterday the director was comparatively unacquainted."

You will use those kinds of skills learned to the extent to which it has been a part of YOUR being! That is, a sympathy of eye and ear, and when-thus attained, can no more be lost or forgotten than the power of speaking!

All experts agree that the most important task for the rehearsal director is to determine what specific musics are to be learned, selected, properly rehearsed and then eventually presented at a concert. Ideally, the music considered should be both playable AND challenging for your young musicians. Therefore, consider carefully all musics for real learning AND musics that are available that will "fit" the abilities of your ensembles.

It is always wise to consider several points:

1. Is the form of the piece workable within the time span available?

2. Is the material suitable for your members? Will the music played be truly enjoyable for your group AND the audience?

3. Do you have sufficient instrumentation that is suitable for the composition selected?

4. Is the technical level of your young musicians sufficient within the context of both rehearsal times (limitations) AND their ability levels?

Is it possible to select a seemingly perfect piece for your BAND, and then discover later that the ability of the group is insufficient to present it as a Concert piece?

WHAT TO DO?

Should you stop rehearsing it? Continue on, anyway? With the inexperienced director/conductor, this "problem" often happens and then the director MUST consider forgoing that specific selection for later in the school year, or even wait until the NEXT school year to continue with it.

PLANNING … *Planning* … PLANNING!

You must use all your resources and skills to make proper

decisions as you select certain materials for your BAND. You must realize that your most valuable asset is adequate rehearsal time!

To properly prepare, consider the number of rehearsals that are truly available, including possible sectional times for practice!

Always factor in that certain rehearsal times might be canceled for ANY reason, many times completely unknown to YOU!

(FACT: My school's basketball team gained the honor of winning sufficient games to go to the State Finals! My principal called for an "all-school assembly" at the same time as my regular rehearsal times! I was not told in advance!! This does happen!)

When you have selected the repertoire you plan to present to your students, you must then develop a structured approach for sufficient rehearsal times. Many ideas might be considered:

"Is it best to analyze the structure read a biography of the composer/arranger to the students. Rehearse the parts one at a time, or, rehearse the entire piece each rehearsal day?"

Always keep the "Big Picture" in mind, even thought it might vary as the rehearsal progress. Always strive for real learning, student-centered times, achievements desired and the development of real and earnestly played musicianship.

Extreme time should be spent on the written dynamics of the music rehearsed. Be absolutely certain that all levels of *"pp"* and *"ff"* are fully understood <u>and played accurately!</u> Insist upon the passages be played with clarity. The decisions you make early in the rehearsal sequences, will be most important later! Be most careful with very loud passages. DO NOT ALLOW BLASTING!

Deep and real teaching occurs when you make the decision to insist upon accurate playing.

You might also consider:

1. How much rehearsal time is actually needed for this particular composition?

2. Are your BAND members actually able to sufficiently

accomplish the selection within the rehearsal times you have selected?

3. Are your BAND members enthusiastically eager about the pieces being rehearsed?

4. Can you instruct the BAND members to adequately play the passages with proper dynamic controls? Don't forget careful phrasing and dynamic controls, also!

At the time the Concert approaches, always play the selected music completely through, from beginning to end. Avoid "spot checking" during the short time prior to the Concert.

Now, should you employ a "theme" to be used at the program? Here are a few examples:

1. Is the music to be played written by a composer from a specific country or nation?

2. You could present an historical anniversary of the piece selected.

3. Plan to play a variety of styles to provide audience pleasure and continued interest.

4. Focus on local and/or regional events possibly connected with the music presented.

5. Present and explain a variety of musical "forms" to further instruct both your students and your audience.

Successful rehearsals are difficult at times, but can be done well as the young director of the school BAND carefully considers all the necessary details. The job of properly directing rehearsals is not an easy one, but thinking carefully and with good planning for the immediate … and … always remember that music participation carries a strong relationship with academic achievement

(see next chapter.)

Other values you are teaching are several which include: artistic, aesthetic, self-affirmation and practical, entertainment, therapeutic, social and economic benefits. YOU are providing many areas of great achievement for your BAND students! Continue to make beautiful music for all of your listeners!

Judgment is the ability to make considered decisions or come to any sensible conclusions. It is discernment, perception, common sense, sharpness, reasoning, wisdom, acuity and astuteness!

Good judgment comes from experience,

and a lot of that comes from bad judgment."

—*Will Rogers, Philosopher*

In conclusion: Lecture your students on the details of any errors you have heard and then corrected! Double check the playing of all "key signatures" and explain the reason and purposes of any changes of keys. If you have sufficient time during rehearsals, offer facts about the life of the composer and/or arranger. Who actually is that person, is that individual still alive and what is expected when you perform the composition? If possible, discover the motivation and/or reason why you have selected the particular piece to be learned and then presented? What will it accomplish when it is formally played at a Concert?

Now, consistently compliment correct playing. Many students do not fully understand what a proper sound actually is for their instrument. Explain it to them! Encourage everyone *(once again}* to keep their jaws down when playing! When you observe a student's embouchure is in error, ask that student to remain after rehearsal time. Schedule a private evaluation and present corrective measures. **Do not wait!** Attack the problem immediately!

The BAND organization must develop active fellowship within the BAND membership to fully organize a full appreciation of their **PRODUCT!**

So, <u>what is</u> the musical product?

Musicality ... emotion ... correct pitches ...

playing in tune ... good breath controls!

Each selection of music must be completely understood for the audience to fully appreciate the presentation! Work always for long phrases. In fact, explain WHY, and then encourage all to mark their music with correct breath marks. Do not ever guess, but help each student-learner to mark the phrases also! Do not guess. So that the BAND students eventually learn that these are some of the most important attributes of the musical product!

Accurate sounds ... with emotional controls are certainly the goals of any musical presentation!

May God bless your product, and always enjoy the comradeship between each of the students as they present their very best efforts! They will remember good playing habits and the excellent training you have given them.

FINALE:

Your BAND members will look to you for directions! Encourage your BAND members daily and actually TELL them specifically what they are doing properly and correctly! Always begin such discussions with what is being played accurately!

My Notes

Chapter Six: **Important Traits**

Now that you have read about some of the situations of a proper BAND rehearsal, we can now discuss the many good and most educational traits that are readily available to the young instrumentalist during any musical encounters.

THERE ARE SEVERAL,
AND MOST IMPORTANT, TRAITS!

CREATIVE: This is most certainly true, and I list it as THE FIRST ONE! Learning to play a musical instrument as a member of any school BAND allows the child to develop his/her personal thinking about many things. The human mind is very malleable, affected by many "outside" sources. Music participation offers the development of the right brain, often ignored in other learning patterns. Given the full opportunity to *"make music happen"* within the framework of a school BAND, the child will develop a yearning for additional learnings! Improvement in school grades often occurs when BAND experiences are introduced to a young learner.

PHYSICAL SKILLS: The manipulation required of the learner to play the intricate keys, valves and sticks of a musical instrument is truly amazing! The young learner quickly develops the muscular skills to actually produce the correct sounds on the various instruments. The intricate following of the written notes develop physical skills so important for many other kinds of manipulations required as an adult.

SOCIAL: The intricate interaction between director and student in BAND is amazingly social! "Getting along" in the BAND room set-up is very obvious to an observer, and the decorum used in rehearsal situations is often noticeable as very "refined" and "quite sociable." Students discuss certain musical passages and ask, "How do YOU do it?"

The inquiries are usually noticed by the BAND director, and many times the director will be asked to solve a specific problem or question. Moving on to Concert decorum and Tour courtesy, the BAND members usually develop an intricately social awareness . . . **an awareness that lasts them for an entire lifetime.**

BEHAVIORAL: BAND discipline, even instrumental discipline, is quickly learned! Position of the instruments at "rest" and then when the director mounts the podium and when the director's arms are listed; are all organized. All are indicated for the correct "instrument holding" behaviors which are to be practiced often. Following THAT procedure, personal behaviors are quickly learned; to follow orders given by the director and then to do the comfortable thing in a social setting. Behaviors quickly learned within the marching BAND system, following the DRUM MAJOR'S baton cues and listening to the specific drum street beat patterns system. Entering the BAND room for a rehearsal quietly and orderly are also behaviors quickly learned as a young BAND member.

CONFIDENCE: is quickly seen when one visits a BAND rehearsal room. The "air" of understanding "what to do" is most clear! Each student finds his/her place, opens their instrument case and begins to "warm up" their lip and mind, to adequately prepare for the rehearsal procedures. The child KNOWS what to do, and does it! The air of "I can do it" permeates the rehearsal room. Even the "shy" or inexperienced BAND member gradually sees others and the confidence trait begins to move about the room! Playing in a Contest setting makes the "confidence" factor very clear. The BAND member knows what to do, and does it! As a judge at many contests, I could always "feel "air of confidence as the BAND would enter the contest room. It is most obvious!

LANGUAGE: Clearly the "Musical Language" is foreign to the child at the beginning. Learning a language is always a "brain function" and the young musician quickly and confidently learns . . . little by little . . . the musical language. Then, the child learns more and more and develops his technique based upon his learning. In fact, science has discovered that the young musician is advanced academically in OTHER subjects . . . all because of his musical understandings! Many times, a certain musical phrase is played and all the young musicians understand that "sound" immediately! The musical language is a catalyst to learning all languages, including English!

PSYCHOLOGICAL: The human mind is so complex that musical learning can take place at the same time as other learnings are occurring! Psychological understandings take place as the child learns to manipulate a musical instrument. I have witnessed amazing successes in BAND experiences. Usually the child's grades in other courses begin to rise, and additional successes are achieved. However, vary rarely and occasionally a young BAND member might suffer serious difficulty in other courses of study. I have gone to the defense of behavioral actions of young musicians who are most successful in BAND experiences, but very undisciplined in other courses. The psychological strain on some child's mind can be quite severe as he/she is trying to learn OTHER subject matter at the same time learning to read music notation.

GLOBAL: This one is not difficult to understand at all! When the musician is introduced to musics of the world, he/she will often develop an interest and perhaps a deep appreciation of that particular style. Style is studied quite often when playing various types of music, and the system often quickly learned and even understood. Differing styles between different countries contribute greatly to global learning. When playing a specific style of music which was introduced to the young musician, the director might use a globe to show and to explain the foreign country's musics! Composers introduce to the young musician musics from many areas of the world and then the musician is exposed to the cultures of those countries. These cultures are then interpreted within the music itself. This is called a "STYLE" of the sounds produced.

TEST TAKING: The concept is quite clear. EVERY piece of music being played is a "test-taking" procedure! When playing music every day, the young musician is taking a "TEST." Learning occurs when the experience matches the brain's interpretation of the symbol. Therefore playing specific notes as the child reads the score placed before him, the child is taking a "test" each and every time a piece of music is being rehearsed, and then performed for an audience. Sight-reading is an experience most directors practice with their student musicians. Reading a selected piece of music **without rehearsing it in advance** is a skill and practice to be readily learned by all musicians. Jazz music form can be an amazing way to learn to improvise the sounds desired (a skill without the written notes available) that is mastered only after years of understanding HOW to practice … the "test" is always in the performance! All musicians should work at this form of "test-taking" … almost daily!

My Notes

Tidbits

Everyday problems that occur in school

BAND rehearsals, presented as "tidbits"

with suggested and plausible solutions.

Tidbit 1:

Problem: BAND students do not observe key changes.

Solution: Do not criticize the BAND, but ask the BAND members to play a major (or minor scale) in the key which was "missed." Play it again in other ways, perhaps soft once and then loudly the next. Always memorized! Then, go back to the piece and play it again. There will always be someone in your BAND who will say, "Hey, we just played a scale in that key!" The problem will be solved each time you use this technique.

Tidbit 2:

Problem: Very poor posture, quite apparent in many sections of your BAND!

Solution: Instruct all BAND members to Stand or Sit straight and when playing their instruments, to keep backs away from the backs of the chairs. Tell and explain fully WHY you are insisting: Lung capacity, proper breath support and good posture are all intertwined.

Now, play the music you were just conducting. When finished, ask the BAND members if it sounded "better" with good posture. Someone will always say "YES" and then explain again why proper breath support and good posture are intertwined.

Tidbit 3:

Problem: Poor tone quality quite apparent from several members of your BAND.

Solution: Talk about pads, valve oil, slide grease, reed controls, etc. This raises an interest in the BAND to "improve" their total sound. Work on Chorales and other tone poems to encourage improvement in the total sound of your BAND. Usually, following a few rehearsals with this stressed, the problem begins to solving itself.

Hooray! The tone concept of your BAND has improved.
Continually encourage THAT sound!

Tidbit 4:

Problem: Percussion students not paying attention; talking amongst themselves, etc.

Solution: Stop the rehearsal and discuss attention that must be given to the process. Discuss the Composer/Arranger's intention(s) as the piece was written. Talk about PRECISION within the entire BAND and (looking at the Percussion section), encourage the Percussion players to watch for your specific conducting directions. Do not discipline them, but focus upon the ENTIRE BAND membership for the necessity of attention to the director and then listening for clarity of the total sound.

Hooray: problem solved for the moment.

Repeat this procedure often until the Percussion section readily and correctly "pay attention" to your conducting and the MUSIC score.

Tidbit 5:

Problem: Baritone Saxophone and Bass Clarinetist players are slouching when playing!

Solution: Discuss with the entire BAND the importance of sitting up straight, with backs away from the chair backs and breathing deeply. Do NOT focus upon the offense or embarrass them in any way. Check the offending student's instrument STANDS for proper adjustment, many times a quick correction will solve the problem.

Tidbit 6:
Problem: BAND members seem to lack full understanding of whole and half steps. Many inaccurate sounds occur during playing of basic scales.
Solution: Assign and then play major/minor scales in SHARP keys. Explain the half steps situation which occurs in EVERY scale to clarify the correct pitches.
Hooray: another problem solved!

Tidbit 7:
Problem: Breath control lacking in the entire FULL BAND.
Solution: Long tones! Play scales with extremely long tones for each pitch. Explain proper and efficient phrasing . . . practice four-bar phrases, perhaps using selections from current BAND literature to explain the entire practice. Ask percussionists to breathe with the BAND as the long phrases are practiced.

Tidbit 8:
Problem: Lack of general stamina from all BAND members. They tire easily!
Solution: Long tones practice is the secret! Play selected passages commenting on phrasing, stamina, and correctness! Have a section play AS THEY STAND, and discuss the problem with others in the BAND. Talk with section leaders privately. Stamina can be learned quickly!

Tidbit 9:
Problem: The students in your young BAND are not careful with their instruments. Many brasses have "stuck slides" and woodwinds may have chipped reeds. Even some percussionists are not using correct sticks/mallets. Many problems seem to be existing!
Solution: Discuss cleanliness and active practice of caring for each instrument. Complete rehearsals a bit early several times

to encourage proper swabbing of the Woodwinds and complete cleaning of the Brass instruments. Talk to the percussionists about keeping the drums and other effects spotless and clean. No writing allowed on drum heads! Explain why!

Tidbit 10:

Problem: Many students do not take their instruments home on the weekends, even when reminded during rehearsals.

Solution: Keep careful record of the names of the students not observing practice at home on weekends! After approximately two weeks begin to discuss the situation of home practice on the weekends. Observe any real changes by checking instruments left in the BAND room for the next several weeks. Praise the students who DO take their instruments home and then explain (again) the necessity of practice ... necessary for consistent improvement ... the real and most important steps to learning musical skills, Make a regular check for several months until the problem is solved.

Tidbit 11:

Problem: After several weeks of rehearsals, you do not hear a general improvement. How to solve THIS one? What to do?

Solution: Discuss what motivation can be achieved as a member of THIS school BAND. Offer incentives to all members and discuss BAND awards to be given at the end of the school year. Group dynamics might be a beginning, Leadership traits can be learned by everyone! Insist upon personal improvement. Teach good listening habits and good practice abilities! Start a "practice chart" system and keep it current!

Tidbit 12:

Problem: Pitch inaccuracies noted seem to be occurring often, seemingly your BAND members do not fully understand the concept of correct and accurate pitch production?

Solution: Ask your Brass players to pull slides and then ask the Woodwinds to pull their mouthpiece and/or barrels out as far as they can. Now play your tuning pitch. LISTEN! Evaluate what is heard, ask each: section: "What do you hear?" Ask all to adjust their instruments to correct positions. LISTEN again! CORRECT? Bring Percussion players into the discussion. Perhaps they can offer opinions? Then discuss ways to correct and to adjust pitches as one is playing. Always LISTEN and _adjust_ to correct pitch level as the playing continues!

Tidbit 13:
Problem: Lack of a real BAND BALANCE during tutti passages.
Solution: Increase the BRASS sound. Explain the dynamic factor, and then ask that all sounds be fully supported with total breath controls. Lessen percussion sound and produce louder all BASS tones. Develop the fullness of balance by increasing third and fourth parts for clarity and accuracy during tutti sounds. Lessen the BASS sound in the Brass sections … work at it … then explain what the audience will hear. Always teach listening carefully … always!

Tidbit 14:
Problem: Flute and Clarinet sections players are very sharp in pitch controls.
Solution: Pull lead pipes and barrels out. Listen to each member play a short passage from a rehearsed piece. Play simple chorales during warm-ups. LISTEN and correct. Discuss pitch accuracy and why it is so necessary for our young BAND.

One Final Comment

The ability to recognize any tone by specific name is called "PER-FECT PITCH." Relative pitch is the ability to accurately recognize (and name) successive pitches after the first one is sounded (as a reference pitch).

We have over 3,000 tiny hairs in the cochlea of our ears, with each vibrating at a differing pitch. The pitch of concert "A," for instance, in the time of HANDEL, vibrated at about 422 cycles per second (1751). In the 1800s, the French composers caused "A" to be raised a bit, to about 430 cps. When Mozart was composing, international agreement finally settled and placed concert "A" at 440 cps.

Students in your BAND who possess a "keen ear" will be troubled when out-of-tune playing is occurring. If each member of a 50-member BAND produced only ONE out-of-tune pitch during any BAND rehearsal, the ears of the director would be bombarded with 44,000 incorrect pitches during each school year! Multiply that fact by the OTHER half steps and many octaves and you will then understand what it takes to be a school BAND director. Work your BAND always to understand fully how to accomplish finally and to properly play all instruments "in tune."

My best to you in your wonderful music career, always!

Dr. Paul Rosene

Postlude

As I completed this discussion of rehearsal procedures and other ideas to improve school BANDS, I was reminded of a special event! Early one school-day morning, I was called by our Superintendent of Schools to tell me that he was coming to our high school early THAT same afternoon and wondered if the school BAND could play? I was thrilled to be asked and I told him that we would be ready when he came.

By the way, I asked, *"What is the occasion?"*

He told me that he was going to plant a tree in the front lawn of our school! That surprised me a bit, but I told him that we would be ready. I went to my Principal's office and told him what had happened. Could the school Band have thirty minutes or so before the event to rehearse? He granted my request, and we were then all organized.

Yes, all organized, I thought, but what in the world would I have the BAND play? *Hmmm.* Well, I was told that he was going to plant a tree … What musics do I have to provide for THAT kind of event. I thought and thought about some kind of music depicting a tree? And then I recalled that I had an arrangement of Kilmer's "TREES" at home, tucked in the piano bench. *Could we somehow create a BAND arrangement?*

Between class periods I ran home to check.

Hooray! There it was! I had it.

Now, my Music Theory class was scheduled to meet the next hour. I had already taught them to write music notation, but could they write the arrangement; could it actually be done? I was very proud of that class. I quickly gathered up score paper. I was ready!

When the class met, I told them what had happened. I wanted them to create a BAND ARRANGEMENT of Joyce Kilmer's "TREES" during this period. I assigned each student to create one specific part for a each instrument of our school BAND. With much encouragement and help to study the piano score, the class members were able to create sufficient BAND parts. *What a surprise for the Superintendent!* The BAND was ready, for I had sufficient time to explain the situation and to rehearse and correct some of the errors we found in the newly created BAND arrangement.

When the Superintendent arrived, I led the BAND playing "TREES!" The Superintendent was completely stunned and totally amazed. The audience, composed of mostly students and a few of the City Officials, applauded the BAND'S endeavors.

When the occasion was completed, the Superintendent asked me, "How in the world did you do that for me today and so quickly?" I explained the particular class activity and the learnings accomplished by each student.

He was thrilled and often spoke of that day in which we provided a musical tribute to our School's Leadership by the playing of Joyce Kilmer's "TREES."

APPENDIX

A Few Music Terms

A few MUSIC <u>TERMS</u> to be memorized and then correctly followed by all student-musicians:

Accelerando – (accel.) Gradually faster
Adagio – Very slow . . . leisurely
Allargando – Gradually slower and louder
Allegretto – Light and cheerful and a bit quicker
Allegro – Lively, brisk, rapid
Andante – Moderately slow, flowing easily
Assai – Very!
Brio – With vigor, life, quick spirit
Crescendo – Gradual increasing in loudness
Da Capo (D.C.) – Repeat from the beginning
Dal Segno (D.S.) – Repeat from the sign
Decrescendo (decres.) – Gradual decreasing in loudness
Dolce – Softly, sweetly, delicately
Fine – The end of the piece
Forte (f) – Moderately loud
Fortissimo (ff) – Loud
Grave – Slow, solemn
Largo– Broadly, slowly
Marcato (marc.) –Accented, and marked
Meno mosso – Less motion, slower
Mezzo-forte (mf) – Moderately loud
Mezzo-piano (mp) – Moderately soft
Morendo – Dying away in tone and time
Pianissimo (pp.) – Extremely soft
Poco a poco – Little by little
Presto – Quickly, faster than allegro
Rallentando (rall.) – Gradually slower
Ritard (rit.) – Gradually slackening in tempo
Vivace – With vivacity, lively, quick

Instrumental Music Vocabulary
Terms Used in Instrumental Music Vocabulary Spelling Test

Anticipation
Applause
Articulation
Audience

Band
Bar
Barrel
Bass Clef
Bell
Bow
Brace
Breath mark
Breath support
Buccinator

Case
Case latch
Casings, valve
Cassette tape
Cheeks
Clarinet
Cleaning cloth
Cornet
Diaphragm
Dotted note
Double bar
Down beat
Duration

Eighth note, rest
Ensemble
Embouchure
Embouchure plate

Exhale
Fermata
Fingertips
Flat
Flute
Foot tap
Forte

Half note, rest
Half step
Harmony
Holes
Horn

Inhale
Instrument

Joint, Foot
Joint, Head
Joint, Lower
Joint, Upper

Keys
Keys signature

Lacquer
Lesson
Ligature
Lines
Lips
Listen
Long tones
Lungs
Measure

Melody
Modiolus
Mouthpiece
Music
Music book
Music stand

Nomenclature
Notes

Orbicularis
    Oris, lower
    and upper
Orchestra

Phrase
Pitch
Piano
Podium
Polishing cloth
Positions
Posture
Percussion
Practice
Preparation

Quarter note, rest
Reed
Repeat
Rest
Rhythm
Rhythm pattern
Rings

Scale
Sharp
Silver
Slide oil

Slide, playing
Slide, tuning
Slur
Song
Spaces
Springs
Staff
Support, breath
Sustained
Swab

Tape recording
Television
Tempo
Tie
Time signature
Tone quality
Tongue
Treble clef
Trombone
Tune-up
Tuning slide

Unison
Up beat
Valves
Valve oil
Videotaping

Warm up
Water key
Whole note, rest
Whole step
Woodwind

Sample Program Organization

Tonight's endeavor has been designed, organized, and rehearsed to appeal to the various tastes of our audiences. The Concert is dedicated to the many Band Boosters who faithfully and untiringly encourage the Schools' Bands.

The Program

PART I

AMPARITO ROCA .... Texidor
A vigorous Spanish March opens tonight's concert with much agitation, movement and melody.

OVERTURE MILITAIRE .... Haydn
This Overture, based on themes from Haydn's Military Symphony, lends itself well to school bands. Arranged by Joseph Skornicka, each section of the band enters with clear melodious passages.

SCHEHERAZADE .... Rimsky-Korsakoff
1. The Sea and Ship of Sinbad
   Flute Cadenza: Sue Hillebrenner
2. The Tale of Prince Kalandar
   Clarinet Cadenza: Rachel Hunter
3. The Young Prince and Princess
   Alto Saxophone Solo: Anna Lee Davis
4. The Festival at Bagdad

PART II

CLARINET CAPERS .... McRae
The familiar melody "Devils Dream" is performed by the entire Clarinet Section. The audience will recognize it as a "Fiddlers" tune, commonly played at square dances.

CHARTREUSE .... Cofield
Miss Anna Lee Davis, Band Vice-President, presents this delightful selection as an Alto Saxophone Solo.

70

Program

MINKA, MINKA .... Frank
    As an encore from Miss Davis, Miss Karen Smith, Alto Saxophonist, and
    Miss Bonnie Claus, Tenor Saxophonist join Ann, forming a Saxophone
    Trio to perform this "Show Piece."

THE LIBERTY BELL .... Sousa
    The Pittsfield High School Concert Band traditionally performs a Sousa
    March to prelude the presentation of the John Philip Sousa Award.

———●———

Presentation of the John Philip Sousa Award for 1959
Mr. Richard Heitholt, Principal, Pittsfield High School
Mrs. Paul F. Grote, Jr., President of the Pittsfield Band Boosters
Mr. Warren Winston, 1958 Sousa Award Recipient

———●———

PART III

SEQUOIA .... LaGassey
    A well written "Tone Painting" describing the massive Sequoia trees found
    in the Western forests of the United States.

BALLET FOR YOUNG AMERICANS .... Hermann
    1. Day Dreaming
        Soloists: Jerry Jones, Trumpet, Leonard Litvan, Clarinet
    2. Prom Nite
        Soloist: Rodney Walker, Cornet
    3. Graduation March

TAMBOO .... Cavez
    An exciting Samba featuring the 1st Flute Section, Sue Hillebrenner, Phyllis
    Peters, Nancy Wendler, and Connie Smith, with background effects by the
    Percussion Section. And Clarinet Cadenza by Leonard Litvan.

BLOCK M .... Bilik
    A stirring Concert March written for the University of Michigan Band,
    is a fitting climax to close the 1959 Spring Concert of the   High
    School Concert Band.

HIGH SCHOOL CONCERT BAND

1st Division Winners State Finals — 1958

Piccolos:

* Hillebrenner, Sue
Peters, Phyllis

Flutes:

Ellis, Judy
* Hillebrenner, Sue
Hittner, Judy
Peters, Phyllis
Smith, Connie
Smith, Janice
Springer, Carol
Wendler, Nancy

Oboes:

Jeffries, Joyce
* Lippincott, Linda 6
Mink, Merrie

Alto Clarinet:

* Burbridge, Lanna 5

Bass Clarinet:

* Rose, Kay 7

Bassoon:

* McHose, Mary

Clarinets:

Athey, Barbara
Ator, Naomi
Atwood, Carole
Barber, Keenan
Baughman, Ruth
Chamberlain, David
* Christian, Joyce
Criss, Carole
Dimond, Jeannie
Dinsmore, Joyce
Evemeyer, Larry
Fulmer, Terry
Hunter, Rachel

Clarinets (cont'd)

Kraybill, Anne
Litvan, Leonard
Robinson, Carolyn
Sloan, Marsha
Smith, Karol
VanderStoep, Linda
Weaver, Carol
Willsey, Sherrie
Tanner, Carole

Alto Saxophones:

Beard, Roger
* Davis, Ann 2
Gleckler, Francis
Loyd, Earl
Smith, Karen
Wood, Nora

Tenor Saxophones:

* Claus, Bonnie
Durr, Dolores 9
McGann, Mary
Orrill, Kathy 9

Baritone Saxophone:

* Shulman, David

French Horns:

* Dean, Vera 3
Evans, Mary 7
Farrell, Peggy
Henry, Bill

Cornets:

Brown, Gilman
Chamberlain, Daniel
Grote, Bill
Jones, Jerry
Schulein, Shirley
Scott, Susan
Vannatta, Dacia

Cornets (cont'd)

* Walker, Rodney 1
Willard, Bob
Zimmerman, Randy

Trumpets:

Duke, George Larry
Grigsby, Lewis

Baritone Horns:

DeHart, Kay 8
Henry, Jackson

Trombones:

Foster, Dale
Fudge, Curtiss
Ingram, Ronnie
Offenbacker, Lowell
Rammazzini, Bob
* Wahlgren, Leland 8
Wilson, Wayne 8

Sousaphones:

* Burbridge, Tom
Smith, Lawrence

Percussion:

Awbrey, David
- Tympani -
* Faris, Gary 4
- Snare Drum -
Ferguson, Janice
- Bass Drum -
Freed Roy
- Snare Drum -
Rutledge, Ann
- Sound Effects -
Seybold, Charles
-Bells -
Stroheker, Lynn
- Cymbals -

1. Band President
2. Vice-President
3. Secretary
4. Treasurer

5. Head Librarian
6. Solo and Ensemble
   Librarian
7. Assistant Librarians

8. Quartermasters
9. In Training
* Section Leader

High School Concert Band School Year 1960–61, Paul E. Rosene, Director

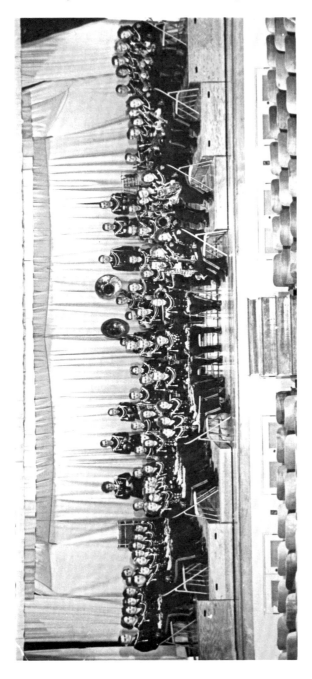

Proposed Seating Chart
for a Young Band

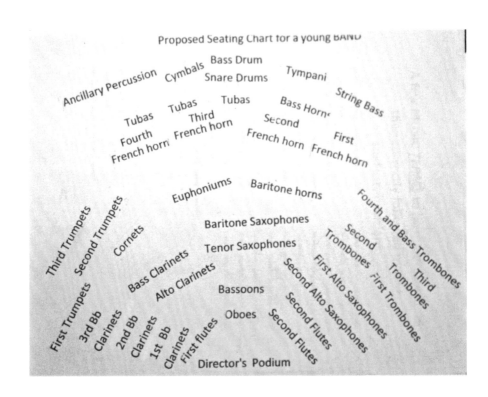

The Junior High School Band, Directed by Mrs. Doris M. Rosene

Marching Band Formation

Pittsfield High School Marching Band

"Community Foundation" Article

Dr. Paul and Doris Rosene Band Fund

How well do you remember your favorite band teacher?

Is it the way they effortlessly, yet masterfully, played a piece of classical music that sticks out in your mind each time you pick up your instrument? Or, is it the way you listen more critically to music; picking out the sound of an individual instrument that your teacher taught you to play?

Great performers are rare. Great teachers of performance are even rarer. That is why former Pittsfield, Illinois band students of Dr. Paul and Doris Rosene have come together to start an Acorn Fund at the Community Foundation, to benefit band participation for years to come and to honor the Rosenes as the musical influences they were.

"When I look back at my time in the band under Dr. Paul Rosene, I remember him always smiling, he was always even-tempered, open minded, and he used to say, 'Any musical experience is worth having once,'" said John Borrowman. Borrowman, Class of 1967, played the cornet in the Pittsfield High School Band, taught under Dr. Paul Rosene. "The memories I have of Rosene and band in Pittsfield, Illinois will always be with me. My hope is that band students today, and in the future, can have those same memories."

78

Dr. Paul Rosene taught at Pittsfield High School from 1957 to 1967. His wife of 69 years, Doris Rosene, also a musical influence in the community, was the band director at Higbee Junior High during that same time.

After Doris' passing in 2020 and as a way to honor the Rosenes, Borrowman along with three other former band members formed a steering committee to put together an effort to encourage and advance student participation in the band program at Pittsfield High School. That steering committee consists of Cherryll Gaffney-Allen, clarinet player in the Class of 1963, John Geisendorfer, cornet player in the Class of 1965, and Dr. Larry Mays, trumpet player in the Class of 1966.

"Even though we were a high school band team, we played and were taught like we were professionals," said Geisendorfer. "The Rosenes raised the musical standards for our small community and introduced us to the worlds of jazz, symphony, movie music, marching music, etc."

Although Dr. Rosene has retired from his music-teaching career, his impact on the Pittsfield community lives on through the Dr. Paul and Doris Rosene Band Fund at the Community Foundation.

Once matured, the Fund will provide direct support for students with financial need who wish to participate in the band program, including tuition for band camps, entrance fees for solo and ensemble contests, and repair or maintenance of student-owned instruments.

"Learning a piece just sections at a time teaches discipline and time management," said Dr. Rosene. "Memorizing and preparing for a recital or contest teaches presentation skills and being in front of an audience. Lastly, practicing teaches dedication and commitment. Through this fund and through endowment, we will provide those life skills to young musicians for generations to come."

Donate to this Fund

"Pike Press" Article

Former students work to memorialize couple that influence the music at Pittsfield schools

By BETH ZUMWALT
Pike Press

Paul and Doris Rosene lived in Pittsfield from 1957-1967 and were the heart of the music programs.

During that time, friendships were forged among band members and four of those former students/ still friends, have joined forces to establish an endowment fund that will deliver, in perpetuity, annual funds to pay for actives of band students Pittsfield High School who have a financial need.

Cheryl Gaffney Allen, Class of 1963 is of Roseville, John Geisendorger, Class of 65 is in North Carolina, John Borrowman, Class of 1967 is in Tennessee and Dr.Larry Mays, Class of 1966 is in Colorado.

The four meet often, via Zoom, and after the death of Doris Rosene last year, decided to raise funds to establish the fund within the parameters of the Community Foundation that serves West Central Illinois and Northeastern Missouri.

"We discussed a scholarship but decided not to go that way because only one person would benefit and we felt there would be years when no band member would be interested in becoming a music teacher," Gaffney-Allen, said." We

Submitted photo

Paul and Doris Rosene were instrumental in the music programs at Pittsfield High School and Higbee Junior High from 1957-1967. A group of former students have raised half of a $15,000 goal to establish an endowment in the couple's name. Paul Rosene lives in Florida, is 91 and still plays trumpet in his church choir. Doris Rosene died last year.

want more than one person to benefit. There are many needy students at Pittsfield High School. The size of the band is around half the size it was when we on the steering committee went to school."With that in mind, the committee is asking for instruments to be donated to the 5th grade band program with the hope that more students would be able to join if an instrument were available. "We're hoping our fund money could pay for an individual's instrument repair, uniform cleaning,

entry fees for solo contest etc,"Gaffney-Alen said. "In addition we're asking for memories , stories, experiences etc from these band memories so I can make a memory book to present to Dr. Rosene."Donors can contribute via credit card at https://www.mycommunityfoundation.org/dr-paul-and-doris-rosene-band-fund, or by check payable to Rosene Fund and mailed to Community Foundation, 4531 Maine Street, Suite A, Quincy, 62305After his time in Pittsfield, Dr.

Rosene accepted a position at Illinois State University where he did significant work in music therapy. He also became known, nationally, for his work with bell choirs. In 1990, the Rosenes retired to Orlando, Fla. Doris Rosene passed away in August 2020. At age 91, Dr. Rosene remains active at his home in Orlando and plays trumpet in his church band.Rosene frequently joins the four former students on their Zoom calls."He's 91, but you wouldn't know it," Gaffney-Allen said.

Courtesy of Beth Zumwalt and Better Newspapers,Inc.

The Author, Dr. Paul E. Rosene

Throughout his long career as a musician/educator, Dr. Rosene has taught at several school and universities, and as well he has led and directed programs in academia and in the U.S. Air Force. In 1967, he joined the faculty at Illinois State University, and he remained as full Professor at the institution until his retirement in 1990. Since then, he has parlayed his experiences into leading and inspiring students as a music consultant to many schools.

Dr. Rosene earned the bachelor of science degree in Music Education from Illinois State University in 1951 and followed that degree with a master degree in Music and Psychology from that institution in 1957. In the intervening years between these two degrees, he served in the U.S. Air Force, becoming a staff sergeant, BAND director, and instructor at the Air Force Band School.

Always committed to his own learning, Dr. Rosene earned the degree of Doctor of Music Education from the University of Illinois in 1976. He is a Certified Master Teacher with the Music Educators National Conference, as well as a Certified Supervisor for Student Teachers in Music and a Certified Master Teacher with the State of Illinois.

He continues, during retirement, with his interest in Handbells and Choirchimes by offering workshops and clinics. He has judged music contests in many states and toured throughout the United States with his University Bands and Handbell/Choirchimes Ensembles.

For his achievements, Dr. Rosene was inducted into the Hall

of Fame from the Illinois State University in 2010 and received the Outstanding Alumnus Awared from the ISU School of Music in 2001 and a Distinguished Service Award in 1990. In 1999, Malmark, Inc. (a handbell company located in Pennsylvania) recognized him with a Service Appreciation Award.

In addition, Dr.Rosene was presented with the Distingished Service Award from the Illinois Music Educators Association in 1991. He has written several Handbell and Choirchimes compositions as well as books and other creative works, including "Special Effects for Handchimes," "Special Effects for Choirchimes Advanced Method" and "Making Music with Choirchimes Instruments."

An unexpected by rewarding perk of his career has been hearing about the many successes of his former students.

Author Dr. Paul E. Rosene

Index

T

U

V

W